|| OM ||

This book is dedicated to my bad habits or bad things in my life and my dream which required me to gain so much knowledge and experience...

"Without Rules/Discipline life is a Dustbin"

The Arya...

DISTRACTED WORLD - DISTRACTED ME | HOW TO BE SUCCESSFUL?

THE FASTEST WAY TO GET SUCCESS IN THIS ERA.

THE ARYA

Contents

Foreword

Do you have big goals in your life and do you want big success? Are you working very hard but not getting any positive response, unable to focus on your goal, dream, or success?

So let me tell you that in this time/age we are living in a hi-tech world, which is constantly reducing our power of focus/concentration.

Because what we used to do in a day/year, today we are doing it in a second, believe that we have come a long way but we have forgotten our inner strength which we got from our God, due to which We have to face failures in fulfilling our goals or dreams.

So let's start reading this book...

In this book, we will know how to achieve success fastly and easy way.

And how to recognize the reasons that are the invisible causes of our failures/unsuccessful and how to overcome them?

As well as knowing those simple or powerful techniques that increase our potential or power and take us to those limits of success quickly.

And more important things. we will learn in the first chapter of the book...

Preface

In this book, we will know all those root causes that hold us to succeeding or failure. Also, know all those advanced fundamentals that need to get succeeding in our life.

First - we will know how to achieve success

Second - we'll go through all those root causes

Third - we will know how to break the distraction or handle it

So, keep reading & along with us.

Acknowledgements

This book is written by me because of my bad habits or bad things in my life and my big dreams which required me to gain so much knowledge and experience.

I have got all this knowledge from books, experience, and successful people. So I would like to give credit for this to him.

Prologue

Hey,

I'm The Arya, I'm an Author, Public Speaker, Trainer, Mentor, Investor, and Businessman.

I am writing this book because I have faced the journey from 0 to 1 in my life and I have seen so many root causes which stop us to achieve success and we keep hope only by looking at successful people. But you are not able to achieve that success and even if you want to do it, we do not know any way to move forward, in this book you will get all those fundamentals that are enough to make you a successful person.

So please forgive me if you find any mistakes. I will try my best to write in easy language and clear form that you can understand

So are you ready to succeed? If ready then start reading...

Warning For You - Disclaimer

Hey, I want to warn you before you read this book because if you read this book, you won't have to leave your friend circle, society's mindset, and your comfort zone, and much more...

So, if you don't want to leave your current society or friend circle, then do not read this book, because it is a fire book on success, and in this book you will find all the steps by which you must achieve success. Because you will not be able to live in this society or this friend circle after you are successful.

You must upgrade your society, or friends circle, where only successful or positive-minded people are available.

So, it depends on what you want.

Success

1

What? Why? And How?

Success, Success, Success

What is success?
How to Achieve it?
What's Your Plan?

What are the things that prevent you to achieve your success? and why?

Are these mental or Physical things?

Write down below. Describe Your success, Goal, Dream, and all the things that you want. What & How do you want? why want? what are the things holding you? & many more....

2

Know Yourself

Success means anything that gives you happiness, which makes you happy, whether it is money or a GF, or to move forward in life, whatever.

Success is the only way to reach your destination or your dream, not success is your dream.

Because no one has a gf, he dreams that I want to have a GF,

Someone has a shop, he has a dream, I want to open a big shopping mall,

A dream can also be something else, whether it is money, power, or a life partner.

Success is a path to enjoyment, we have to touch on that point...

So let's go to the chapter, find the purpose of your life or know yourself means what is the main purpose of your own life or how to find and recognize, I have already told so much Rama-Gatha, still, let's go To know further how to find or identify the purpose of your life.

So let me ask you a question,

- What is that thing that holds a very important place in your life?
- What is that thing that grooms or upgrades your life?
- What is that thing that gives you value, respect, and power? (Whether it will be valid for some or not for some)
- What is that one thing for which you can give an hour out of your important time?

- What is that thing for which you spend your day? year? Can you live full life?

  If still not found then proceed further...

- What is that thing, while doing which your hunger, thirst, and fatigue all remain away?
- What is that thing for which you have to go where you want to do this throughout the day? And you will not get food? nor water? No money will be given? So what would you like to do?
- What is the one thing you can sacrifice yourself for?

Note down all the answers on a paper and what will come out the most in front of you is your passion or purpose of life or that is you...

3

How to get to your original version

Before starting the chapter I want to tell you a story.

Look, a long time ago a farmer lived and farmed and ran his house, he had two children, **Changu and Mangu** (the name is fictitious, it has nothing to do with any person or thing) or I do not intend to anyone. To offend the person, if the name of any article/person matches, it will be considered as a mere coincidence, it will not have anything to do with the author, publication nor any legal action will be valid.

So the farmer's age was gradually increasing and he was getting old, one day he went to his field with both his bulls, and he started to rest after plowing a round, but he did not notice that his both the bulls are open and while resting, he started sleeping and he slept in the shade of the tree, after a while he woke up and saw that both my bulls were missing, so he got upset. And he started searching, searching - it was evening, his bulls could not find him.

So he went home after giving up, went home and told the whole story to his two sons, and also told him that there is a forest at a short distance from the field, if possible, you can get the same bulls because I also did bulls from there in my childhood. Brought that which was lost by me in childhood, and I have scoured the whole farm-barn and village, the bulls has not been found.

And the father said to the sons that if the two of you will find them, then I will get him married to a beautiful girl... ha... ha... enjoy the story...

So yesterday morning both of them went towards the forest early in the morning and reached the forest but after searching for a long time they could not find the bulls, it has been day to since morning, they neither eaten, nor drink anything and they were working hard without rest. . After a long time, Changu speaks,

"Hey Mangu will not meet bulls get back at home now"

Mangu - You go, I will see, if I do not meet, I will come.

Changu - ok.

Mangu kept searching - searching, and went to the middle of the forest, when it was evening from the day, he also started getting scared, but only two thoughts were running in his mind, 1st - that of marrying a beautiful girl. , and the second bulls would be found in the forest itself, which was told by his father and it was his command, and it was the profits of his pure life, because of which it was his duty to find the bulls.

So it was going to be night from the evening, as he was entering in the middle of the forest and was getting scared, and in the same way this thought was going to stir up more and more in his mind, due to which he returned back. didn't want to go

Then after walking for some time after nightfall, he found a cave, and he was afraid to go into the cave but he dared to enter the cave and entered the cave,

What was to happen then, along with his two bullocks, there were a number of bulls, goats, and cows, which, after getting lost in the forest, used to hide in this cave, then in the morning, all the cows, goats, bulls were one Tied with a rope and left for the house, as soon as he was leaving the house, it was as if a procession of animals was going through the forest. So many blazing lines which was made by animals.

And from morning to day, he reached his village, and as soon as he reached his village, he went to his house, after going home he tied all the animals at his house and fed them.

Then his father was shocked to see all this that he had sent both his sons to find his bullocks, how did he bring so many animals, so Mangu told the whole story that he found a cave in the middle of the forest, in which this All the animals were one, due to which I brought them all.

After some time that farmer became the biggest man of the village, who had maximum number of animals in the village.

And he got his second son married to the most beautiful girl in the village. Due to this Mangu also became very happy and started living his life happily.

So if you have read the whole story well, then answer these questions in your own language first and then read my answer.

What was the purpose of Mangu - Bringing the bull

How to get it - go to the forest

Why, 1st. Because his father had once brought back his oxen from the forest, (means you can follow the path of those who have already done something in your steam)

2nd. And his father also told that he has searched the whole village, farm, barn.(Means you can also learn from those who have lost, in your steam, who have tried all the things but have not been able to reach because of their own effort, is - not getting bullock.)

Goal or Dream - marry a beautiful girl

Success - Bringing Bullock

So tell me why only Mangu brought why Changu could not bring,

When the purpose of both was the same, the path was also the same, dream and success were also the same, but why only Mangu, why not Changu?

Look, the biggest thing with Changu, neither did he have the patience nor did he believe in himself.

Due to this, he went back from the cave.

What would have happened if Mangu had also searched from morning to day, from day to evening and from evening to night and without eating and drinking, even after getting tired of searching, even if he reached near the cave and came back without entering the cave without fear, what would have happened, remained as it was, but he captured his fears and emerged victorious.

Many times, we can't even control our fear after doing everything and end up back before we can even enter the cave of our destination.

We will meet challenges you every step of the way, it is our job to stay focused on your goal and your dream and make victory by defeating every difficulty and fear.

There are many such people,

1st. Who neither have their destination,

2nd. Even if it did, they wouldn't have a way to reach their dream

3rd. Even if it happens, he is unable to go there because of fear and problems.

4rth. Even if we went on defeating him, some would have come back after walking some distance (due to patience and more hard work and faith), like Changu had returned from morning to day.

5th. If those who reach even close to their destination, they fall behind the cave or cave of success. Because of one big leap and one last biggest fear, whatever it may be.

6th. Those who enter the cave are successful. And become successful people in front of us.

The same happens with us, when everyone has his own dream, there is a way, but even after working hard, we accept everything, and start cursing him, and who has his own and his own dreams believed, he believes in his life only by achieving his dreams.

So if you have a dream, you want success then you have to forget yourself first, I say you have to believe that you are dead... I am afraid, trouble, nothing happens, I am dead. No one else can kill me, my dream, success has killed me, I am in possession of that. No matter what happens, I will continue to fight - I will continue to fight. Whatever happens, I will not go back, I am dead, I am in pain, nothing to sell, I have sacrificed myself for my dream.

So who are you, you have to decide - Changu or Mangu....

Look, the guru mantra to achieve success is simple.

1st. Find the purpose of your life.

Know yourself why God has sent you to this earth, what do you want to do, what do you want to be. And how do you want to live your life?

2nd. believe on it.

Believe in yourself and your dream, and keep moving towards your goal.

and 3rd. Focus on that and take massive action till you get success.

Keep imagining and visualize your dream and take massive action for it till you get that dream or that success.

That's it, the guru mantra to get success in life... and if you want to know it clearly, then you can read our second book - "The Covert Key to Success", which will help you to reach your destination in your life. I will help a lot. That's why I named it - "The Complete Bible of Success".

To get success, you have to become a stone, no matter what happens, I will leave it only after achieving it. Even if I die or die, but I will keep on finding him.

"And the bigger your dream, the bigger your success, and the bigger the success, the bigger the struggle."

So be ready, to cross this river of fire, then you will find your heaven.

So let's know in the next chapter how to believe on your dreams and yourself...

Believe means to believe in yourself and your dreams, to believe in yourself that I can, I will,It is my responsibility to do it, whatever it is, I will show it.

Because it doesn't take us long to do what we believe in

What we can think we can do, I say you can do fast what you believe in

So how to believe and how to increase the power of your faith.

Look, you have to do two things to believe it.

Remind yourself daily what is your goal or your dream.

And secondly, live it in the now or live from now on, as if that thing has happened now, you are the check on that thing, you are what it is.

So let me give you a simple formula to do it.

1st. Live Future in Present

Daily You have to do this simple thing, after waking up in the morning, give 5 minutes to your goal or your dream and imagine it, how then? Look choose a peaceful place to fulfill your dreams and sit here, and write down on a paper your goal or dreams what you want to do or want, then think you have got it, how did you get it, think those paths Imagine, visualize those little steps that you have given to make your dreams come true, look at everyone how you did it, when you did it, and see that you have reached there, and sound out of your mind that you are in the same place Pay now, what are you doing now and how are you doing?

Then go in front of your mirror and say, whatever you have to do,

Example - like "I am the best seller author in this world" and then breathe in, and exhale

It can also be related to you, health, wealth, career or life partner.

Health - "I am the healthiest person, I have no problem, I am fit.

Wealth - "I am the richest person, I do daily deals of lakhs, crores, billions of rupees, and earn money in the night or at sleeping.

Life Partner - my husband or wife is beautiful, sexy, hot or whatever (according to you), and she makes me happy

After that sit quietly for 5 minutes, and then go on with your daily work.

2nd. Taking in the body

whenever you are breathing water or food, (with any of these you can use your dream) speak or think these words at that time

This is what happens? it is registered in your subconscious mind, and you are also informing your body that I am this and I have reached the point by which you are going to strengthen your own belief, so that You don't have to face many difficulties in achieving your goal or dream

Like, when I say time to drink water, I take a choke when I have a glass of water in my hand, then I say/think - "I am a best seller author" Then I take another choke.

As I drink water, I speak like that, and whenever I drink, I do it

By which it gets stored in my mind and body, and it increases my power to believe,

And it also gives this message to this universe,

If I drink water 10 times a day then how many times do I speak or think, like 20-30 times approx.

If the universe will get this mails 20 to 30 times a day, will it not support us?

a very good dialogue from a very good film by Shahrukh Khan

"If you want anything with all your heart, the whole universe is engaged in bringing you to it."

Sometimes these Bollywood people also say a lot, but we think that it is only entertainment, we never pay attention to it.

So if you want to unleash more faith power or want to achieve your goal faster then you can also read my second book - **"The Covert Key to Success"** which will help you to achieve your goal

Will learn in the next chapter - focus till you do not get success...

5

Focused on it until not get success

Focused till you do not get success - means you will have to be fully focused on the goal of your dream, till you do not take to achieve the goal.

"While doing, the roots of practice are visible; rope goes on the mark even on a stone as soon as it comes." This

couplet means that by continuous practice any unskilled person can become skilled - from Sant Kabir.

Focused means not only focusing on your goal, but you also have to take massive actions with it.

What do you have to do, how to do it, when? Break it all down into daily/monthly and yearly tasks and go about taking action on a large scale - without giving up until you get tired of it.

You can do this as Kaizen (Japanese secret - Kaizen is a Japanese word meaning change for the better or continuous improvement).

Let me explain kaizen secrets first - look when you are given a bundle of wood to break together will you not break it, just given one by one you will break them all, this is what kaizen tells To reach your dream, make small goals and break them.

As I explain to you with an example,

My goal is to be a best seller and best author. So will I become just by thinking and believing or will I have to do something?

If it has to be done then how?

My annual goal is to write 2 books,

My half yearly goal is to write 1 book

My quarterly goal is - to complete half the book

That's how my monthly goal was to write about 50 pages

So the goal of the daily goal - writing 1 to 2 pages minimum

Just if I write 1 to 2 pages daily, then all my goals and dreams will be fulfilled. It is so easy, isn't it, so this is called taking action on a large scale, which means taking action in harmony towards your goal.

"Means to keep searching in the woods till both the ballets are found, whether it is morning to day, day to evening, or evening to night. - From the story Changu and Mangu."

You can do this, you can use the one thing in your life, and one thing for now, - from one thing book.

Example - One thing in my life - Bestseller author.

One thing for now - 1 to 2 pages of writing.

This gives me inspiration and I will start writing that one to two pages and finish it too.

And definitely ask yourself this question when taking your massive action - **"Am I doing this with my full potential? Am I giving my best?"**

It will keep improving and increasing in your work, and you will keep moving forward.

If you want to know more about how to stay focused and fully focused on your goals and keep moving forward, then you can read our second book - **"The Covert Key to Success"**.

We will learn in the next chapter - about distraction...

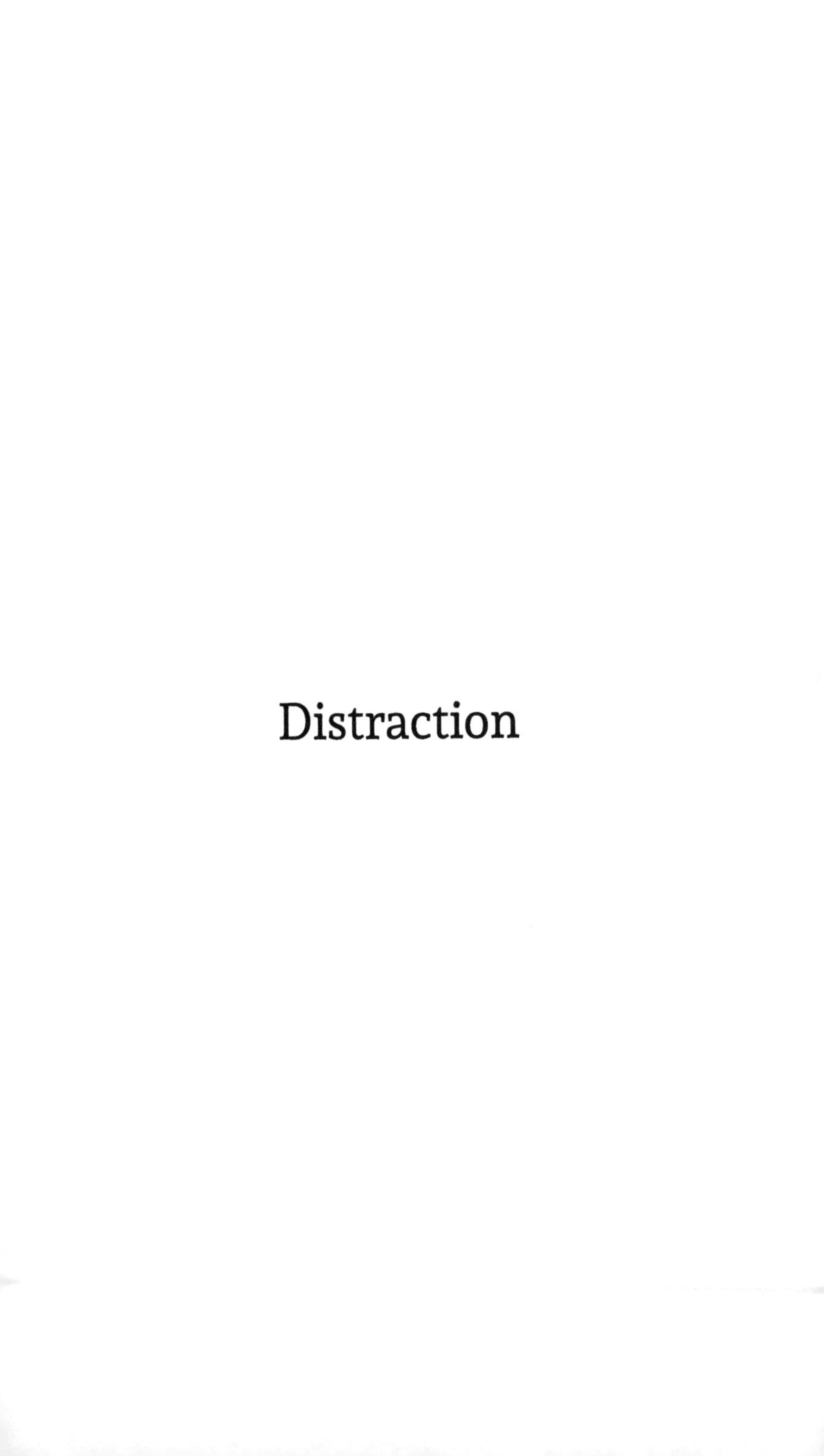

Distraction

6

Know Your Distraction

Distraction - Distraction - Distraction - Everything is the world; Distraction is Distraction.

Today's era is just a spectacle, everywhere you will definitely see the sight, whether it is in the form of advertisement, or in the form of distracting someone.

Due to which you are not able to concentrate on your goal or your dream and get lost in your path. You are attracted to others by seeing, hearing, and wanting to be like them.

Distraction means - something that takes your attention away from what you were doing or thinking.

Types of Distraction:

1st. Internal

This is the effect of your own thoughts, while doing or doing some work, start thinking about something else, without completing that task, getting engaged in some other work. You might call this "thinking too much", etcetera.

2nd. external

It distracts you in 4 ways

1) by ear - by hearing
2) by eye
3) by touch
4) by taste

Distraction Ways

Now in this age, first of all social media, internet, or technology is the main key to distractions.

And second my own friend circle, family, or crush (any pretty girl/guy who is attracted to you) is another key to distraction

Distraction is the biggest disease in today's era, we are not doing anything. Due to which we are becoming lazy.

Due to this, all the diseases are getting accumulated in our body, and we are not able to do anything.

As soon as we wake up, we start using the phone and social media, we start watching TV. Just like there is nothing else in life,

If you look at the children of today, they cannot go to school, college without the phone, and if you scroll through their phone, you will find new-upgraded versions of games and social media apps etc.

Is this life???

This social media is a poison wire for us - which without seeing us hollowing out, eroding our inner power.

Due to which we are not able to focus our attention on one thing. And don't want to bother.

And keep falling in their clutches.

So you find your destruction, and write on those one paper, which destruction is destructing you, internal or external, write full details about it.

Let us go ahead how to get out of those distractions or work on them....

7

How to Overcome from it

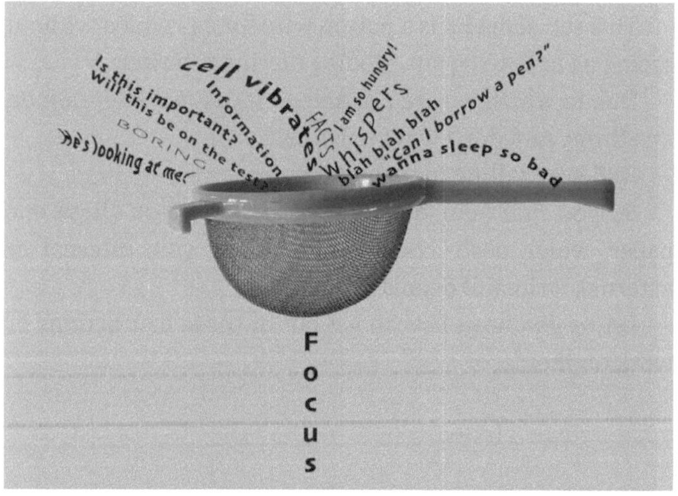

How to overcome distractions - Look, to avoid distractions, a monkey has to come out of the mouth of a crocodile, we must have read the story in childhood that how a monkey comes out of the mouth of a crocodile with its cleverness. Similarly, to avoid distraction is to get out of the mouth of a crocodile,

So I am telling you some tips or tricks by which you can stop your distraction but it depends on you how you use them,

The first biggest problem - first of all, start keeping your phone away from you, like - touch only when there is important work, otherwise do not touch,

Strictly stop using social media, I remember I have uploaded only one to two posts on my social media account so far, because... because if I had uploaded the post, I would have been confused. I keep checking how many likes, how many messages are sent etc. I haven't opened my social media for about 5 months, you won't find any social media apps on my phone. Why, because I don't want my time to be wasted or become a victim of distraction.

2nd - stop making friends of befaltoo, and stop passing time with friends, you will get thousands of friends, you can make friends whenever you want, friends kill your important time and become a victim of distraction in the timepass affair becomes. For example, if you are doing important work, your friend called you - let's go to a movie today man, what will you do, you will leave your important work and go to see the film, what will happen to life There will be no effect in me, but if you have done your important

work at that place, then today you would have crossed a straight path to reach your goal.

3rd. Stop multitasking and focus on one thing - first, you stop multitasking, you will find many people who say that you have no time, who say that by doing two things at a time, you look productive, and you will soon Your goals will be met.

I ask - "Can you be a voice on two boats at a time" No, if you do two jobs or more at a time, you don't belong anywhere, you will be scattered

Suppose two housewives - first one is preparing dal and rice two at a time, and the other is preparing one by one, then will the food of two housewives have the same taste, not what they are making one by one? That is, their food will be better and their food will taste more, because they focused their attention on only one thing at a time, and cooked together with love, others focused their attention on both, due to which the taste of their food changed. Gone was the neglect of the earlier one, this housewife must have been born very well.

It means to focus on one thing - when you are doing some work, then you are only doing it and not any other work, even if it is a small task.

For example, when you are studying, you are only reading and not even operating the phone, eating food, or talking to someone, etc.

When you are eating, you are only eating, not talking.

4rth. Silence - Silence means when you feel that I am getting distracted, just be silent and absorb it and don't do anything. When you are free, start doing something.

5th. Watch Motivational Movies, Shows, Podcasts, or Videos - You can watch motivational movies, shows, podcasts, or videos in your spare time that inspire you, and inspire you to achieve your goals and dreams.

6th. Listen to your favorite songs - or you can listen to an inspiring, motivational, or song of your choice that will change your mood and re-focus on your goal or your work.

7th. Meditation - Meditation is very important in today's world because today we work less with our body but do more with our mind, every man collects the garbage of the day in his mind and causes stress and anxiety in his

life. Prey.

And just as exercise or yoga is necessary to keep your body and muscle fit, meditation is very important for your mind.

Meditation is very simple, you understand that this is a child's play, but the more you keep it simple and easy, the better it is for you, instead of meditation, you can also do this - Vipassana meditation, which can be done. Mahatma Buddha has discovered, otherwise, you can also follow Sadhguru or you can follow my simple and easy way.

It is like this, sit on one of your peace palaces with a simple waist straight and slowly take the breath and release it and slowly close your eyes and focus only on the breath. It can be as late as you can, eg - 5 minutes, 10 minutes, 15 minutes, or 30 minutes, etc.

But you should go on increasing it according to your age and not decreasing it.

Like - suppose my age is 30 years now - then I should use it for 30 minutes which will remove all the garbage from my mind, and I will feel happiness, peace, and spirituality.

Whoever is 40, must use 40 minutes, but if you are just starting then you may have to face a little problem, but do not break your courage and keep your spirits up.

Some days there will be problems but gradually you will start seeing improvement, and you will start feeling happiness, peace, and happiness in your life.

It is better if you do it mainly in the morning or evening, because at that time the atmosphere is calm, and you will not have to face much trouble in doing it but whenever you have free time you can do it at that time.

8th. exercise, walk, or play - exercise is also a very important thing in your life, as I have also mentioned above that meditation is very important for your mind and exercise your body, in today's time whether it is a girl or she Yes, it is equally necessary for all.

Question - So can I do it even when I am upset?

Answer - Sure, you can do it, you can do it whenever you get time, if you want, you can play any sport instead of exercise, but your body must exercise.

Playing or walking or exercising - all three are the same thing, which keeps your body fit, and gives you the agility

You can also do the gym or dance instead, it depends on you what you like to do.

According to me, if you are 20 to 40 years old, you can walk, along with going to the gym (you can also dance) would be best for you.

If you are over 40 then you can do walking, yoga, pranayama, and exercise.

But I am not saying that you cannot, but exercise is very important for your body in today's era.

9th. Laughing - Laughter also works as a boon for our life, laughter is a very important thing for us, it activates the muscles in your mouth, and gives us freedom from dreadful diseases like stress and anxiety.

To laugh you do not need to see any place and time, you can laugh whenever you want, no reason or reason is needed for this.

Let me tell you that for people who are very serious about themselves, you will see that the brightness on their face is decreasing and you will also see the lack of meat in their body and they are getting old very quickly.

Whatever he eats, he will not feel in his body "meaning he will not be able to keep himself happy and he will soon become a victim of stress and anxiety" I have seen many such people who consider themselves harsh and serious, that is why they are the only ones in these are victims of diseases.

So laughing is also very important in life, and you can also see next to you that you will get to see the glow on the face and bodies of the people who live, whatever you say to them, there will be no effect on them. They take the biggest decisions quickly, no stress and worry can ever bother them.

But in today's time society and our job and friend circle, all themselves are becoming serious and doing us too.

Have we ever wondered why we survived when we were kids? Because we used to laugh - we used to play.

But now we are becoming young or Buddha and just keep thinking that we wish we were children, this stress or life problem does not bother us, we keep enjoying our life well.

I ask you - "So can't we be kids today"

please answer me....tell me the answer.

Let me tell you we can still become children today, get rid of our stress, worry, and problems in life, and can reach our goals easily. How...

It is simple, when we are left, we play - used to chuckle, in the same way, still play and litter, and laugh and enjoy the journey of this life.

Due to this you will enjoy your food and your body and face will also glow and you will enjoy your life happily.

So if you want to achieve your dream of success quickly and easily then you can also read our second book - "The Covert Key to Success".

We will learn about the conclusion in the next chapter.

Conclusion

So girls and boys this is their conclusion first of all, what? Why? and how? Find outAnd then start your journey from the simple directions mentioned and enjoy those heights of your destination.And if someone is bothering you, then you can also remove them by using the tricks of discussion and enjoy life.Just read the book completely, no one can stop you from reaching your goal.

Thank You

Thank you :)

To read this book in its entirety.

You have known the basic mantra of success that can change your life, you can get what you want, whatever you want,

So enjoy your life and achieve your success.

If you want, you can also read our second book on success,

"The Covert Key to Success"

And if you want to save, increase and multiply money in life then you can also read our finance-related post,

"The First Book of Investing Ever!!!"

And if you want, you can also connect with us on our youtube channel, where you can connect with us through live sessions, and share your views and your issue on which we will conclude and solve it together

Youtube Channel Name or ID - The Arya Show

Thank U :)

9 798888 051054

Printed by Libri Plureos GmbH in Hamburg, Germany